Easy Ketogenic Diet for Beginners

A Tasty and Easy Cookbook To Enjoy Your Delicious Low Carb Ketogenic Recipes

Juliana Diaz

TABLE OF CONTENTS

SMOOTHIES & BREAKFAST

Breakfast Chaffle Sandwich

Preparation Time: 10 minutes

Cooking Time: 10 minutes

Serving: 1

Ingredients:

- 2 basics cooked chaffles
- Cooking spray
- 2 slices bacon
- 1 egg

Method:

1. Spray your pan with oil.
2. Place it over medium heat.
3. Cook the bacon until golden and crispy.
4. Put the bacon on top of one chaffle.
5. In the same pan, cook the egg without mixing until the yolk is set.
6. Add the egg on top of the bacon.
7. Top with another chaffle.

Nutritional Value:

- Calories 514
- Total Fat 47 g
- Saturated Fat 27 g
- Cholesterol 274 mg
- Sodium 565 mg
- Potassium 106 mg
- Total Carbohydrate 2 g

- Dietary Fiber 1 g
- Protein 21 g

Total Sugars 1 g

Stuffed Jalapenos

Preparation Time: 10 minutes Cooking Time: 15
minutes

Serve: 12

Ingredients:

- 1/2 cup chicken, cooked and shredded
- 6 jalapenos, halved
- 3 tbsp green onion, sliced
- 1/4 cup cheddar cheese, shredded
- 1/2 tsp dried basil
- 1/4 tsp garlic powder
- 3 oz cream cheese
- 1/2 tsp dried oregano
- 1/4 tsp salt

Directions:

- Preheat the oven to 390 F.
- Mix all ingredients in a bowl except jalapenos.

- Stuff chicken mixture into each jalapeno halved and place on a baking tray.
- Bake for 25 minutes.
- Serve and enjoy.

Nutritional Value (Amount per Serving):

Calories 106

Fat 9 g

Carbohydrates 2 g

Sugar 1 g

Protein 7 g

Cholesterol 35 mg

Quick & Easy
Blueberry Chaffle

Preparation Time: 15 minutes Servings: 2

Ingredients:

- 1 egg, lightly beaten

- 1/4 cup blueberries

- 1/2 tsp vanilla

- 1 oz cream cheese

- 1/4 tsp baking powder, gluten-free

- 4 tsp Swerve

- 1 tbsp coconut flour

Directions:

1. Preheat your waffle maker.

2. In a small bowl, mix coconut flour, baking powder, and Swerve until well combined.

3. Add vanilla, cream cheese, egg, and vanilla and whisk until combined.

4. Spray waffle maker with cooking spray.

5. Pour half batter in the hot waffle maker and top with 4-5 blueberries and cook for 4-5 minutes until golden brown. Repeat with the remaining batter.

6. Serve and enjoy.

Nutrition: Calories 135 Fat 8.2 g
Carbohydrates 11 g Sugar 2.6 g
Protein 5 g Cholesterol 97 mg

Apple Cinnamon Chaffles

Preparation Time: 20 minutes Servings: 3

Ingredients:

- 3 eggs, lightly beaten

- 1 cup mozzarella cheese, shredded

- ¼ cup apple, chopped

- ½ tsp monk fruit sweetener

- 1 ½ tsp cinnamon

- ¼ tsp baking powder, gluten- free

- 2 tbsp coconut flour

Directions:

1. Preheat your waffle maker.

2. Add eggs in a mixing bowl and beat until frothy.

3. Add remaining ingredients and stir until well combined.

4. Spray waffle maker with cooking spray.

5. Pour 1/3 of batter in the hot waffle maker and cook for 4 minutes or until golden brown. Repeat with the remaining batter.

6. Serve and enjoy.

Nutrition: Calories 142 Fat 7.4 g
Carbohydrates 9.7 g Sugar 3 g
Protein 9.6 g Cholesterol 169 mg

Sweet Vanilla Chocolate Chaffle

Preparation Time: 10 minutes Servings: 1

Ingredients:

- 1 egg, lightly beaten

- 1/4 tsp cinnamon

- 1/2 tsp vanilla

- 1 tbsp Swerve

- 2 tsp unsweetened cocoa powder

- 1 tbsp coconut flour

- 2 oz cream cheese, softened

Directions:
1. Add all ingredients into the small bowl and mix until well combined.

2. Spray waffle maker with cooking spray.

3. Pour batter in the hot waffle maker and cook until golden brown.

4. Serve and enjoy.

Nutrition: Calories 312 Fat 25.4 g
Carbohydrates 11.5 g Sugar 0.8 g
Protein 11.6 g Cholesterol 226 mg

Mozzarella Peanut Butter Chaffle

Preparation Time: 15 minutes Servings: 2

Ingredients:

- 1 egg, lightly beaten

- 2 tbsp peanut butter

- 2 tbsp Swerve

- 1/2 cup mozzarella cheese, shredded

Directions:

1. Preheat your waffle maker.

2. In a bowl, mix egg, cheese, Swerve, and peanut butter until well combined.

3. Spray waffle maker with cooking spray.

4. Pour half batter in the hot waffle maker and cook for 4 minutes or until golden brown. Repeat with the remaining batter.

5. Serve and enjoy.

Nutrition: Calories 150 Fat 11.5 g
Carbohydrates 5.6 g Sugar 1.7 g
Protein 8.8 g Cholesterol 86 mg

Peanut Butter Sandwich Chaffle

Preparation Time: 15 minutes Servings: 1

Ingredients:

For chaffle:

- **1 egg, lightly beaten**

- **1/2 cup mozzarella cheese, shredded**

- **1/4 tsp espresso powder**

- **1 tbsp unsweetened chocolate chips**

- **1 tbsp Swerve**

- **2 tbsp unsweetened cocoa powder**

For filling:

- **1 tbsp butter, softened**

- **2 tbsp Swerve**

- **3 tbsp creamy peanut butter**

Directions:

1. Preheat your waffle maker.

2. In a bowl, whisk together egg, espresso powder, chocolate chips, Swerve, and cocoa powder.

3. Add mozzarella cheese and stir well.

4. Spray waffle maker with cooking spray.

5. Pour 1/2 of the batter in the hot waffle maker and cook for 3-4 minutes or until golden brown. Repeat with the remaining batter.

For filling:

1. In a small bowl, stir together butter, Swerve, and peanut butter until smooth.

2. Once chaffles is cool, then spread filling mixture between two chaffle and place in the fridge for 10 minutes.

3. Cut chaffle sandwich in half and serve.

Nutrition: Calories 190 Fat 16.1 g
Carbohydrates 9.6 g Sugar 1.1 g
Protein 8.2 g Cholesterol 101 mg

Cherry Chocolate Chaffle

Preparation Time: 10 minutes Servings: 1

Ingredients:

- 1 egg, lightly beaten

- 1 tbsp unsweetened chocolate chips

- 2 tbsp sugar-free cherry pie filling

- 2 tbsp heavy whipping cream

- 1/2 cup mozzarella cheese, shredded

- 1/2 tsp baking powder, gluten-free

- 1 tbsp Swerve

- 1 tbsp unsweetened cocoa powder

- 1 tbsp almond flour

Directions:

1. Preheat the waffle maker.

2. In a bowl, whisk together egg, cheese, baking powder, Swerve, cocoa powder, and almond flour.

3. Spray waffle maker with cooking spray.

4. Pour batter in the hot waffle maker and cook until golden brown.

5. Top with cherry pie filling, heavy whipping cream, and chocolate chips and serve.

Nutrition: **Calories 264 Fat 22 g**
Carbohydrates 8.5 g Sugar 0.5 g
Protein 12.7 g Cholesterol 212 mg

Pulled Pork Chaffle Sandwiches

Preparation Time: 20 minutes Cooking Time: 28 minutes
Servings: 4

Ingredients:

- 2 eggs, beaten

- 1 cup finely grated cheddar cheese
- ¼ tsp baking powder

- 2 cups cooked and shredded pork

- 1 tbsp sugar-free BBQ sauce

- 2 cups shredded coleslaw mix

- 2 tbsp apple cider vinegar

- ½ tsp salt

- ¼ cup ranch dressing

Directions:

1. Preheat the waffle iron.

2. In a medium bowl, mix the eggs, cheddar cheese, and baking powder.

3. Open the iron and add a quarter of the mixture. Close and cook until crispy, 7 minutes.

4. Transfer the chaffle to a plate and make 3 more chaffles in the same manner.

5. Meanwhile, in another medium bowl, mix the pulled pork with the **BBQ** sauce until well combined. Set aside.

6. Also, mix the coleslaw mix, apple cider vinegar, salt, and ranch dressing in another medium bowl.

7. When the chaffles are ready, on two pieces, divide the pork and then top with the ranch coleslaw. Cover with the remaining chaffles and insert mini skewers to secure the sandwiches.

8. Enjoy afterward.

Nutrition: Calories 374 Fats 23.61g Carbs 8.2g Net Carbs 8.2g Protein 28.05g

Simple Ham Chaffle

Time: 15 minutes Serve: 2

Ingredients:

- 1 egg, lightly beaten

- 1/4 cup ham, chopped
- 1/2 cup cheddar cheese, shredded

- 1/4 tsp garlic salt

For Dip:

- 1 1/2 tsp Dijon mustard

- 1 tbsp mayonnaise

Directions:

1. Preheat your waffle maker.

2. Whisk eggs in a bowl.

3. Stir in ham, cheese, and garlic salt until combine.

4. Spray waffle maker with cooking spray.

5. Pour half of the batter in the hot waffle maker and cook for 3-4 minutes or until

golden brown. Repeat with the remaining batter.

For Dip:

1. In a small bowl, mix mustard and mayonnaise.

2. Serve chaffle with dip.

Nutrition: Calories 205 Fat 15.6 g
Carbohydrates 3.4 g Sugar 0.9 g
Protein 12.9 g Cholesterol 123 mg

Delicious Bagel Chaffle

Time: 15 minutes Serve: 2

Ingredients:

- 1 egg, lightly beaten

- 1/4 tsp garlic powder

- 1/4 tsp onion powder

- 1 1/2 tsp bagel seasoning

- 3/4 cup mozzarella cheese, shredded

- 1/2 tsp baking powder, gluten-free

- 1 tbsp almond flour

Directions:

1. Preheat your waffle maker.

2. In a bowl, mix egg, bagel seasoning, baking powder, onion powder, garlic powder, and almond flour until well combined.

3. Add cheese and stir well.

4. Spray waffle maker with cooking spray.

5. Pour 1/2 of batter in the hot waffle maker and cook for 5 minutes or until golden brown. Repeat with the remaining batter.

6. Serve and enjoy.

Nutrition: Calories 85 Fat 5.8 g
Carbohydrates 2.4 g

Sugar 0.5 g Protein 6.6 g Cholesterol 87 mg

Asian Garlic

Chicken

Preparation Time: 10 minutes Cooking Time: 4 Hours
Serve: 6

Ingredients:

- 1 1/2 lbs chicken breasts, skinless and boneless
- 2 tbsp water
- 2 tbsp soy sauce
- 1/2 onion, chopped
- 1 1/2 tsp red pepper flakes
- 2 garlic cloves, minced
- 1/2 tsp ground ginger

Directions:

1. Place chicken into the crockpot.
2. Add remaining ingredients on top of chicken.
3. Cover and cook on high for 4 hours.
4. Shred the chicken using a fork and serve.

Nutritional Value (Amount per Serving):

Calories 250

Fat 9 g

Carbohydrates 10 g

Sugar 6 g

Protein 34 g

Cholesterol 100 mg

PORK, BEEF & LAMB RECIPES

Pork Egg Roll Bowl

Preparation Time: 10 minutes Cooking Time: 10 minutes Serve: 6

Ingredients:

- 1 lb ground pork
- 3 tbsp soy sauce
- 1 tbsp sesame oil
- 1/2 onion, sliced
- 1 medium cabbage head, sliced
- 2 tbsp green onion, chopped
- 2 tbsp chicken broth
- 1 tsp ground ginger
- 2 garlic cloves, minced
- Pepper
- Salt

Directions:

1. Brown meat in a pan over medium heat.

2. Add oil and onion to the pan with meat. Mix well and cook over medium heat.

3. In a small bowl, mix together soy sauce, ginger, and garlic.

4. Add soy sauce mixture to the pan.

5. Add cabbage to the pan and toss to coat.

6. Add broth to the pan and mix well.

7. Cook over medium heat for 3 minutes.

8. Season with pepper and salt.

9. Garnish with green onion and serve. **Nutritional Value (Amount per Serving):** Calories 171

Fat 5 g

Carbohydrates 10 g

Sugar 5 g

Protein 23 g

Cholesterol 56 mg

Roasmary Garlic Pork Roast

Preparation Time: 10 minutes Cooking Time: 1 hour 10 minutes

Serve: 6

Ingredients:

- 4 lbs pork loin roast, boneless
- 4 garlic cloves, peeled
- 2 lemon juice
- 1/4 cup fresh sage leaves
- 1/3 cup fresh rosemary leaves
- 1 tbsp salt

Directions:

1. Add sage, rosemary, garlic, lemon juice, and salt into the blender and blend until smooth.
2. Rub herb paste all over roast and place on hot grill.
3. Grill for 1 hour.
4. Sliced and serve.

Nutritional Value (Amount per Serving):

Calories 655

Fat 30 g

Carbohydrates 5 g

Sugar 1 g

Protein 88 g

Cholesterol 246 mg

SEAFOOD & FISH RECIPES

Garlic Shrimp with Goat Cheese

Serves: 4

Prep Time: 30 mins

Ingredients

- 4 tablespoons herbed butter

- Salt and black pepper, to taste

- 1 pound large raw shrimp

- 4 ounces goat cheese

- 4 garlic cloves, chopped

Directions

1. Preheat the oven to 3750F and grease a baking dish.
2. Mix together herbed butter, garlic, raw shrimp, salt and black pepper in a bowl.
3. Put the marinated shrimp on the baking dish and top with the shredded cheese.
4. Place in the oven and bake for about 25 minutes.
5. Take the shrimp out and serve hot.

Nutrition Amount per serving

Calories   294 To-

tal Fat 15g 19%

Saturated Fat 8.9g 44%

Cholesterol 266mg 89%

Sodium 392mg 17%

Total Carbohydrate 2.1g 1%

Dietary Fiber 0.1g 0%

Total Sugars 0.8g

Protein 35.8g

Grain Free Salmon Bread

Serves: 6

Prep Time: 35 mins

Ingredients

- ½ cup olive oil

- ¼ teaspoon baking soda

- ½ cup coconut milk

- 2 pounds salmon, steamed and shredded

- 2 pastured eggs

Directions

1. Preheat the oven to 3750F and grease a baking dish with olive oil.
2. Mix together coconut milk, eggs, baking soda and salmon in a bowl.
3. Pour the batter of salmon bread in the baking dish and transfer into the oven.
4. Bake for about 20 minutes and remove from the oven to serve hot.

Nutrition Amount per serving

Calories 413

Total Fat 32.4g 42% Saturated Fat 8.5g 42% Cholesterol 138mg 46%

Sodium 143mg 6%

Total Carbohydrate 1.5g 1% Dietary Fiber 0.4g 2%

Total Sugars 0.7g

Protein 31.8g

Garlic Parmesan Cod

Serves: 6

Prep Time: 35 mins Ingre-

dients

- 1 tablespoon extra-virgin olive oil

- 1 (2½) pound cod fillet

- ¼ cup parmesan cheese, finely grated

- Salt and black pepper, to taste

- 5 garlic cloves, minced

Directions

1. Preheat the oven to 4000F and grease a baking dish with cooking spray.
2. Mix together olive oil, garlic, parmesan cheese, salt and black pepper in a bowl.
3. Marinate the cod fillets in this mixture for about 1 hour.
4. Transfer to the baking dish and cover with foil.
5. Place in the oven and bake for about 20 minutes.
6. Remove from the oven and serve warm.

Nutrition Amount per serving

Calories 139 Total Fat 8g 10%

Saturated Fat 1.7g 8%

Cholesterol 37mg 12%

Sodium 77mg 3%

Total Carbohydrate 1g 0%

Dietary Fiber 0.1g 0% Total Sugars 0g

Protein 16.3g

Salmon with Sauce

Preparation Time: 10 minutes Cooking Time: 3
minutes

Serve: 4

Ingredients:

- 1 lb salmon
- 1/2 lemon juice
- 1 tbsp garlic, minced
- 1 tbsp Dijon mustard
- 1 tbsp dill, chopped
- 1 tbsp mayonnaise
- 1/3 cup sour cream
- Pepper
- Salt

Directions:

1. Preheat the oven to 425 F.
2. In a bowl, mix together sour cream, lemon juice, dill, Dijon, and mayonnaise.
3. Place salmon on baking tray and top with garlic, pepper, and salt.
4. Pour half sour cream mixture over salmon.
5. Cover and bake for 20 minutes. Uncover and bake for 10 minutes more.

6. Serve with remaining sauce.

Nutritional Value (Amount per Serving):

Calories 213

Fat 12 g

Carbohydrates 3.1 g

Sugar 0.3 g

Protein 23 g

Cholesterol 59 mg

MEATLESS MEALS

Rutabaga Noodles

Preparation Time: 10 minutes Cooking Time: 10

minutes

Serve: 4

Ingredients:

- 25 oz rutabaga, peel, cut and spiralized using slicer
- 1/2 tbsp chili powder
- 1/3 cup olive oil
- 1/2 tsp garlic powder
- ¼ tsp onion powder
- 1 tsp salt

Directions:

1. Preheat the oven to 450 F.
2. Add all ingredients into the large bowl and toss well.
3. Spread rutabaga mixture on a baking

tray and bake for 10 minutes.

4. Serve and enjoy.

Nutritional Value (Amount per Serving):

Calories 150

Fat 17 g

Carbohydrates 2 g

Sugar 0.6 g

Protein 0.4 g

Cholesterol 0 mg

SOUPS, STEWS & SALADS

Coconut Squash

Soup

Preparation Time: 10 minutes Cooking Time: 25

minutes

Serve: 8

Ingredients:

- 3 cups butternut squash, chopped
- 2 garlic cloves, chopped
- 1 tbsp coconut oil
- 1 tsp dried onion flakes
- 1 ½ cups unsweetened coconut milk
- 1 tbsp curry powder
- 4 cups vegetable stock
- 1 tsp kosher salt

Directions:

1. Add squash, coconut oil, onion flakes, curry powder, stock, garlic, and salt into a large saucepan. Bring to boil.
2. Turn heat to medium and simmer for 20 minutes.
3. Puree the soup using a blender until smooth.
4. Return soup to the saucepan and stir in coconut milk

44

and cook for 2 minutes.

5. Serve and enjoy.

Nutritional Value (Amount per Serving):

Calories 145

Fat 12 g

Carbohydrates 10 g

Sugar 3 g

Protein 2 g

Cholesterol 0 mg

Cheese Mushroom Shrimp Soup

Preparation Time: 10 minutes Cooking Time: 15 minutes Serve: 8

Ingredients:

- 24 oz shrimp, cooked
- 8 oz cheddar cheese, shredded
- ½ cup butter
- 1 cup heavy cream
- 32 oz vegetable stock
- 2 cups mushrooms, sliced
- Pepper
- Salt

Directions:

1. Add stock and mushrooms to a large pot. Bring to boil.
2. Turn heat to medium and add cheese, heavy cream, and butter and stir until cheese is melted.
3. Add shrimp. Stir well and cook for 2 minutes more.
4. Serve and enjoy.

Nutritional Value (Amount per Serving):

Calories 390

Fat 28 g

Carbohydrates 3 g

Sugar 0.8 g

Protein 30 g

Cholesterol 17

mg

BRUNCH & DINNER

Coconut Kale Muffins

Preparation Time: 10 minutes Cooking Time: 30 minutes

Serve: 8

Ingredients:

- 6 eggs
- 1/2 cup unsweetened coconut milk
- 1 cup kale, chopped
- ¼ tsp garlic powder
- ¼ tsp paprika
- 1/4 cup green onion, chopped
- Pepper
- Salt

Directions:

1. Preheat the oven to 350 F.
2. Add all ingredients into the bowl and whisk well.
3. Pour mixture into the greased muffin tray and bake in oven for 30 minutes.
4. Serve and enjoy.

Nutritional Value (Amount per Serving):

Calories 92

Fat 7 g

Carbohydrates 2 g

Sugar 0.8 g

Protein 5 g

Cholesterol 140 mg

Blueberry Muffins

Preparation Time: 10 minutes Cooking Time: 25

minutes

Serve: 12

Ingredients:

- 2 eggs
- ½ tsp vanilla
- 1/2 cup fresh blueberries
- 1 tsp baking powder
- 6 drops stevia
- 1 cup heavy cream
- 2 cups almond flour
- 1/4 cup butter, melted

Directions:

1. Preheat the oven to 350 F.
2. Add eggs to the mixing bowl and whisk until well mix.
3. Add remaining ingredients to the eggs and mix well to combine.
4. Pour batter into greased muffin tray and bake in oven for 25 minutes.
5. Serve and enjoy.

Nutritional Value (Amount per Serving):

Calories 190

Fat 18 g

Carbohydrates 6 g

Sugar 1.4 g

Protein 5.4 g

Cholesterol 55 mg Coconut Bread

DESSERTS & DRINKS

Fruit Salad

Protein Peanut

Butter Ice Cream

Preparation Time: 5 minutes Cooking Time: 5 minutes Serve: 2

Ingredients:

- 5 drops liquid stevia
- 2 tbsp heavy cream
- 2 tbsp peanut butter
- 2 tbsp protein powder
- ¾ cup cottage cheese

Directions:

1. Add all ingredients into the blender and blend until smooth.
2. Pour blended mixture into the container and place in refrigerator for 30 minutes.
3. Serve chilled and enjoy.

Nutritional Value (Amount per Serving):

Calories 222

Fat 15 g

Carbohydrates 7 g

Sugar 2 g

Protein 16 g

Cholesterol 27 mg

BREAKFAST RECIPES

Mini Bacon

Guacamole Cups

Serves: 4

Prep Time: 40 mins

Ingredients

- 1 ripe avocado
- 9 bacon slices, 6 slices halved, and 3 slices quartered
- 2 tablespoons onion, minced
- Kosher salt and black pepper, to taste
- 1 small jalapeno, seeded and minced

Directions

1. Preheat the oven to 4000F and turn 4 mini-muffin pans upside down on a baking sheet.
2. Spray the tops of the overturned muffin tins and place the quarter of the slice on top.
3. Wrap the sides of the mini-muffin pans with the longer portions of bacon and secure with a toothpick.
4. Bake for about 25 minutes and remove carefully from the mini muffin cups.
5. Meanwhile, mash avocado with a fork in a medium bowl and stir in the jalapeno, onions, salt and black pepper.

6. Put the guacamole in the bacon cups and serve warm.

Nutrition Amount per serving

Calories 337

Total Fat 27.7g 36%

Saturated Fat 7.9g 40% Cholesterol 47mg 16%

Sodium 991mg 43%

Total Carbohydrate 5.6g 2% Dietary Fiber 3.6g

13% Total Sugars 0.6g

Protein 16.9g

APPETIZERS & DESSERTS

Garlicky Green Beans Stir <u>Fry</u>

Serves: 4

Prep Time: 25 mins

Ingredients

- 2 tablespoons peanut oil

- 1 pound fresh green beans

- 2 tablespoons garlic, chopped

- Salt and red chili pepper, to taste

- ½ yellow onion, slivered

Directions

1. Heat peanut oil in a wok over high heat and add garlic and onions.

2. Sauté for about 4 minutes add beans, salt and red chili pepper.

3. Sauté for about 3 minutes and add a little water.

4. Cover with lid and cook on low heat for about 5 minutes.

5. Dish out into a bowl and serve hot.

Nutrition Amount per serving

Calories   107 Total Fat 6.9g 9%

Saturated Fat 1.2g 6% Cholesterol 0mg 0%

Sodium 8mg 0%

Total Carbohydrate 10.9g 4% Dietary Fiber 4.3g 15%

Total Sugars 2.3g Protein 2.5g

Collard Greens with Burst Cherry Tomatoes

Serves: 4

Prep Time: 25 mins

Ingredients

- 1 pound collard greens
- 3 strips bacon, cooked and crisped
- ¼ cup cherry tomatoes
- Salt and black pepper, to taste
- 2 tablespoons chicken broth

Directions

1. Put the collard greens, cherry tomatoes and chicken broth in a pot and stir gently.
2. Cook for about 8 minutes and season with salt and black pepper.
3. Cook for about 2 minutes and stir in the bacon.
4. Cook for about 3 minutes and dish out into a bowl to serve hot.

Nutrition Amount per serving

Calories 110
Total Fat 7.6g 10% Saturated Fat 2.3g 11%
Cholesterol 0mg 0%
Sodium 268mg   12%
Total Carbohydrate 6.7g 2% Dietary Fiber 3.9g
14% Total Sugars 0.3g
Protein 5.7g

PORK AND BEEF RECIPES

Garlic Rosemary Pork Chops

Serves: 4

Prep Time: 30 mins

Ingredients

- 1 tablespoon rosemary, freshly minced
- 2 garlic cloves, minced
- 4 pork loin chops
- ½ cup butter, melted
- Salt and black pepper, to taste

Directions

1. Preheat the oven to 3750F and season pork chops with salt and black pepper.
2. Mix together ¼ cup butter, rosemary and garlic in a small bowl.
3. Heat the rest of the butter in an oven safe skillet and add pork chops.
4. Sear for about 4 minutes per side until golden and brush pork chops generously with garlic butter.
5. Place skillet in the oven and bake for about 15 minutes until cooked through.

6. Dish out and serve hot.

Nutrition Amount per serving

Calories 465

Total Fat 43g 55% Saturated Fat 22.1g 110% Cholesterol

130mg 43%

Sodium 220mg 10%

Total Carbohydrate 1.1g 0% Dietary Fiber 0.4g 1%

Total Sugars 0g Protein 18.4g

.

Zesty Pork Chops

Serves: 4

Prep Time: 50 mins

Ingredients

- 4 tablespoons butter
- 3 tablespoons lemon juice
- 4 pork chops, bone-in
- 2 tablespoons low carb flour mix
- 1 cup picante sauce

Directions

1. Coat the pork chops with low carb flour mix.
2. Mix picante sauce and lemon juice in a bowl.
3. Heat oil in a skillet on medium heat and add the chops and picante mixture.
4. Cook covered for about 35 minutes and dish out to serve hot.

Nutrition Amount per serving

Calories 398

Total Fat 33.4g 43% Saturated Fat 15g 75%

Cholesterol 99mg 33%

Sodium 441mg 19%

Total Carbohydrate 4g 1% Dietary Fiber 0.7g 3%

Total Sugars 2.1g

Protein 19.7g

SEAFOOD RECIPES

Broccoli and Cheese

Serves: 4

Prep Time: 20 mins

Ingredients

- 5½ oz. cheddar cheese, shredded
- 23 oz. broccoli, chopped
- 2 oz. butter
- Salt and black pepper, to taste
- 4 tablespoons sour cream

Directions

1. Heat butter in a large skillet over medium high heat and add broccoli, salt and black pepper.
2. Cook for about 5 minutes and stir in the sour cream and cheddar cheese.
3. Cover with lid and cook for about 8 minutes on medium low heat.
4. Dish out to a bowl and serve hot.

Nutrition Amount per serving

Calories 340

Total Fat 27.5g 35% Saturated Fat 17.1g 85%

Cholesterol 77mg 26%

Sodium 384mg 17%

Total Carbohydrate 11.9g 4% Dietary Fiber 4.3g 15%

Total Sugars 3g Protein 14.8g

CHICKEN AND POULTRY RECIPES

Cheesy Chicken Tenders

Serves: 6

Prep Time: 35 mins

Ingredients

- 1 cup cream
- 4 tablespoons butter
- 2 pounds chicken tenders
- Salt and black pepper, to taste
- 1 cup feta cheese

Directions

1. Preheat the oven to 3500F and grease a baking dish.
2. Season chicken tenders with salt and black pepper.
3. Heat butter in a skillet and add chicken tenders.
4. Cook for about 3 minutes on each side and transfer to the baking dish.
5. Top with cream and feta cheese and place in the oven.
6. Bake for about 25 minutes and remove from the oven to serve.

Nutrition Amount per serving

Calories 447

Total Fat 26.4g 34% Saturated Fat 13.1g 65%

Cholesterol 185mg 62%

Sodium 477mg   21%

Total Carbohydrate 2.3g 1% Dietary Fiber 0g 0%

Total Sugars 1.8g Protein 47.7g

Air Fried Chicken

Serves: 2

Prep Time: 20 mins

Ingredients

- 1 tablespoon olive oil
- 4 skinless, boneless chicken tenderloins
- 1 egg
- Salt and black pepper, to taste
- ½ teaspoon turmeric powder

Directions

1. Preheat the air fryer to 3700F and coat the fryer basket with olive oil.
2. Beat the egg and dip the chicken tenderloins in it.
3. Mix together turmeric powder, salt and black pepper in a bowl and dredge chicken tenderloins.
4. Arrange the chicken tenderloins in the fryer basket and cook for about 10 minutes.
5. Dish out on a platter and serve with salsa.

Nutrition Amount per serving

Calories 304

Total Fat 15.2g 20% Saturated Fat 4g 20%

Cholesterol 179mg 60%

Sodium 91mg 4%

Total Carbohydrate 0.6g 0% Dietary Fiber 0.1g 0%

Total Sugars 0.2g Protein 40.3g

BREAKFAST RECIPES

Easy Chia Seed Pudding

Total Time: 10 minutes Serves: 4

Ingredients:

- ¼ tsp cinnamon
- 15 drops liquid stevia
- ½ tsp vanilla extract
- ½ cup chia seeds
- 2 cups unsweetened coconut milk

Directions:

1. Add all ingredients into the glass jar and mix well.
2. Close jar with lid and place in refrigerator for 4 hours.
3. Serve chilled and enjoy.

Nutritional Value (Amount per Serving): Calories 347; Fat 33.2 g; Carbohydrates 9.8
g; Sugar 4.1 g; Protein 5.9 g; Cholesterol 0 mg;

Grain-free

Overnight Oats

Total Time: 10 minutes Serves: 1

Ingredients:

- 2/3 cup unsweetened coconut milk
- 2 tsp chia seeds
- 2 tbsp vanilla protein powder
- ½ tbsp coconut flour
- 3 tbsp hemp hearts

Directions:

1. Add all ingredients into the glass jar and stir to combine.
2. Close jar with lid and place in refrigerator for overnight.
3. Top with fresh berries and serve.

Nutritional Value (Amount per Serving): Calories 378; Fat 22.5 g; Carbohydrates 15 g; Sugar 1.5 g; Protein 27 g; Cholesterol 0mg;

LUNCH RECIPES

Avocado Cabbage Salad

Total Time: 20 minutes Serves: 4

Ingredients:

- 2 avocados, diced
- 4 cups cabbage, shredded
- 3 tbsp fresh parsley, chopped
- 2 tbsp apple cider vinegar
- 4 tbsp olive oil
- 1 cup cherry tomatoes, halved
- 1/2 tsp pepper
- 1 1/2 tsp sea salt

Directions:

1. Add cabbage, avocados, and tomatoes to a medium bowl and mix well.
2. In a small bowl, whisk together oil, parsley, vinegar, pepper, and salt.
3. Pour dressing over vegetables and mix well.
4. Serve and enjoy.

Nutritional Value (Amount per Serving): Calories 253; Fat 21.6 g; Carbohydrates 14 g; Sugar 4 g; Protein 3.5 g; Cholesterol 0 mg;

Creamy Garlic Onion Soup

Total Time: 45 minutes Serves: 4

Ingredients:

- 1 onion, sliced
- 4 cups vegetable stock
- 1 1/2 tbsp olive oil
- 1 shallot, sliced
- 2 garlic clove, chopped
- 1 leek, sliced
- Salt

Directions:

1. Add stock and olive oil in a saucepan and bring to boil.
2. Add remaining ingredients and stir well.
3. Cover and simmer for 25 minutes.
4. Puree the soup using an immersion blender until smooth.
5. Stir well and serve warm.

Nutritional Value (Amount per Serving): Calories 90; Fat 7.4 g; Carbohydrates 10.1 g; Sugar 4.1 g; Protein 1 g; Cholesterol 0 mg;

DINNER RECIPES

Cauliflower Couscous

Total Time: 25 minutes Serves: 4

Ingredients:

- 1 head cauliflower, cut into florets
- 14 black olives
- 1 garlic cloves, chopped
- 14 oz can artichokes
- 2 tbsp olive oil
- 1/4 cup parsley, chopped
- 1 lemon juice
- 1/2 tsp pepper
- 1/2 tsp salt

Directions:

1. Preheat the oven to 400 F/ 200 C.
2. Add cauliflower florets into the food processor and process until it looks like rice.
3. Spread cauliflower rice on a baking tray and drizzle with olive oil. Bake in preheated oven for 12 minutes.
4. In a bowl, mix together garlic, lemon juice, artichokes, parsley, and olives.
5. Add cauliflower to the bowl and stir well. Season with pepper and salt.
6. Serve and enjoy.

Nutritional Value (Amount per Serving): Calories 116; Fat 8.8 g; Carbohydrates 8.4 g; Sugar 3.3 g; Protein 3.3 g; Cholesterol 0 mg

Zucchini Soup

Total Time: 20 minutes Serves: 8

Ingredients:

- 2 ½ lbs zucchini, peeled and sliced
- 1/3 cup basil leaves
- 4 cups vegetable stock
- 4 garlic cloves, chopped
- 2 tbsp olive oil
- 1 medium onion, diced
- Pepper
- Salt

Directions:

1. Heat olive oil in a pan over medium- low heat.
2. Add zucchini and onion and sauté until softened. Add garlic and sauté for a minute.
3. Add vegetable stock and simmer for 15 minutes.
4. Remove from heat. Stir in basil and puree the soup using a blender until smooth and creamy. Season with pepper and salt.
5. Stir well and serve.

Nutritional Value (Amount per Serving): Calories 62; Fat 4 g; Carbohydrates 6.8 g; Sugar 3.3 g; Protein 2 g; Cholesterol 0 mg;

DESSERT RECIPES

Quick Chocó Brownie

Total Time: 10 minutes Serves: 1

Ingredients:

- 1/4 cup almond milk
- 1 tbsp cocoa powder
- 1 scoop chocolate protein powder
- 1/2 tsp baking powder

Directions:

In a microwave-safe mug blend together baking powder, protein powder, and cocoa.

1. Add almond milk in a mug and stir well.
2. Place mug in microwave and microwave for 30 seconds.
3. Serve and enjoy.

Nutritional Value (Amount per Serving): Calories 207; Fat 15.8 g; Carbohydrates 9.5 g; Sugar 3.1 g; Protein 12.4 g; Cholesterol 20 mg;

BREAKFAST RECIPES

Sausage Patties

No traditional breakfast would be complete without sausage patties. Packed with protein, these would be wonderful before your morning run.

Total Prep & Cooking Time: 20 minutes Level: Beginner

Makes: 4 Patties

Protein: 25 grams Net Carbs: 5.2 grams Fat:

9 grams

Sugar: 1 gram

Calories: 272

What you need:

- 1/3 tsp onion powder

- 3/4 lb. ground pork

- 1/3 tsp salt

- 4 3/4 oz. mushrooms, chopped

- 1/3 tsp garlic powder

- 4 oz. kale, thinly sliced

- 1/8 tsp ground ginger

- 2 tbs coconut oil, separated

- 1/8 tsp nutmeg

- 2 garlic cloves, minced

- 1/4 tsp fennel seeds

Steps:

1. Melt 1 tablespoon of coconut oil in a skillet.

2. Put in the mushrooms, minced garlic and kale and stir fry for approximately 5 minutes and remove from heat.

3. In a dish, combine the ground pork, cooked vegetables, onion powder, garlic powder, nutmeg, and fennel seeds.

4. Divide into 4 sections and create patties by hand.

5. In the same skillet, pour a tablespoon of coconut oil and heat.

6. Fry the patties for approximately 2 minutes and turn over to brown the other side. Flip over as necessary to fully cook the meat in the middle of the patties.

7. Serve immediately and enjoy.

Variation Tip:

You can choose to mix up the recipe using different meat or vegetables such as ground turkey or beef and spinach or bell peppers.

LUNCH RECIPES

Spicy Cauliflower

Turkey

This moist dish will keep you satisfied throughout the day and have you coming back
for seconds at dinnertime.

Total Prep & Cooking Time: 25 minutes Level: Beginner

Makes: 4 Helpings

Protein: 23 grams Net Carbs: 4.4 grams

Fat: 24 grams

Sugar: 0 grams

Calories: 310

What you need:

- 3/4 tsp salt

- 12 oz. ground turkey

- 3/4 tbs mustard

- 1 2/3 cups cauliflower

- 3/4 tsp pepper

- 2 tbs coconut oil

- 3/4 tsp thyme

- 1 tsp onion powder

- 3/4 tsp salt

- 2 cloves garlic

- 3/4 tsp garlic powder

- 1 2/3 cups coconut milk, full fat

- 3/4 tsp celery salt

Steps:

1. Pulse the cauliflower florets in a food blender for approximately 1 minute on high until crumbly.

2. Heat the cauliflower in a saucepan.

3. Scoop the cauliflower into a tea towel and twist to remove the moisture, repeating as necessary until as much of the water is removed as possible.

4. Heat a large pot and melt the coconut oil.

5. Mince the garlic and pour into the hot pot to simmer for approximately 2 minutes.

6. Combine the ground turkey to the garlic and brown for about 7 minutes, stirring with a wooden scraper to break up the meat.

7. Blend the riced cauliflower, salt, thyme, garlic powder, celery salt, mustard, and pepper with the meat until combined.

8. Reduce the temperature and finally add the coconut milk. Simmer for approximately 6 additional minutes.

9. Serve hot and enjoy!

Variation Tips:

- If you continue to reduce the dish by half and it will

become thicker and can be served as a dip at your next party.

- Alternatively, you can use ground pork, lamb or beef with this recipe. You can also add other vegetables such as broccoli.

- Optional garnishes include bacon, cherry tomatoes, hot sauce or jalapenos.

SNACK RECIPES

Pigs in a Blanket

Take a trip back your childhood with this fun low carb snack and even better if you get the kids to help!

Total Prep & Cooking Time: 40 minutes Level: Beginner

Makes: 4 Helpings (3 Corn Dogs per serving)

Protein: 7 gram Net Carbs: 3 grams Fat:

26 grams

Sugar: 1 gram

Calories: 278

What you need:

- 1/8 cup heavy cream

- Coconut oil spray

- 1/8 tsp salt

- 8 oz. almond flour

- 1/8 tsp garlic powder

- 3 tsp coconut flour

- 1/8 tsp onion powder

- 3/4 tsp baking powder, gluten-free

- 1/8 tsp pepper

- 3 tbs butter, salted and melted

- 1 large egg

- 2 beef hot dogs
- 1/8 cup water

Steps:

1. Set the oven to heat at 350° Fahrenheit. Use the coconut oil spray to lightly grease a mini cupcake tin.
2. In a big dish, whip the garlic powder, pepper, coconut flour, onion powder, and baking powder together removing any lumpiness.
3. Combine the eggs, almond flour, water, butter, heavy cream, and salt and totally incorporate the batter.
4. Let the mixture sit for approximately 3 minutes as it slightly thickens.
5. Evenly distribute into the prepped tin.
6. Slice each hot dog 6 times and place a piece into each of the poured dough.
7. Heat for approximately 20 minutes and remove to the counter.
8. Wait about 10 minutes before serving.

Baking Tip:

Consider using beef or organic hot dogs for this recipe as conventional hot dogs usually have unwanted additives.

DINNER RECIPES

Egg Roll Bowl

Take out is not a thing of the past when you have this recipe to make in your own kitchen. And you do not even have to tip.

Total Prep& Cooking Time: 20 minutes

Level: Beginner

Makes: 4 Helpings

Protein: 29 grams Net Carbs: 1 gram

Fat: 27 grams

Sugar: 0 grams

Calories: 376

What you need:

- 16 oz. ground sausage
- 1/2 tbs onion powder
- 4 cloves garlic, minced
- 1 tbs ginger, minced
- 4 cups cabbage, shredded
- 2 tsp tamari sauce, gluten-free
- 8 oz. mushrooms, sliced
- 1 tbs toasted sesame oil

Steps:

1. Brown the sausage in a non-stick skillet, crumbling the meat

with a wooden spatula.

2. Combine the onion powder, ginger, tamari sauce, and garlic and stir for approximately 60 seconds.

3. Blend the mushrooms and cabbage into the skillet and blend with the spatula for about 3 additional minutes.

4. Remove from the burner and season with toasted sesame oil.

5. Serve immediately and enjoy!

Baking Tip:

1. If you do not want to shred the cabbage yourself, you can use store bought shredded cabbage. Make sure there are not carrots included if you do not want to raise the carbs in the recipe.

Variation Tip:

1. Substitute ground beef or turkey for variety.

2. You can add a fried or boiled egg to the top of this salad if you need to raise your protein macros for the day.

UNUSUAL DDELICIOUS MEAL RECIPES

Salmon Tartare

This would be the Keto diet's version of raw fish sushi in this mini fat bomb that will have you smacking your lips.

Total Prep & Cooking Time: 25 minutes plus 2 hours to marinate (optional)

Level: Intermediate

Makes: 4 Helpings

Protein: 28 grams Net Carbs: 1.8 grams

Fat: 40 grams

Sugar: 0 grams

Calories: 272

What you need:

- 16 oz. salmon fillet, skinless
- 5 oz. smoked salmon
- 1/4 tsp cayenne pepper
- 4 oz. mayonnaise, sugar-free
- 1/4 cup parsley, chopped
- 4 oz. extra virgin olive oil
- 2 tbs lime juice
- 1 tbs caper brine
- 2 tbs green olives, chopped

- 1/4 tsp pepper
- 2 tbs capers, chopped
- 1 tsp mustard, dijon

Steps:

1. Slice the smoked and fresh salmon into cubes about 1/4 inch wide and toss into a glass dish.
2. Blend the mayonnaise, cayenne pepper, chopped olives, pepper and mustard with the salmon until combined thoroughly.
3. Finally integrate the parsley, olive oil, lime juice, capers, and caper brine until incorporated fully.
4. Layer plastic wrap over the bowl and refrigerate for approximately 2 hours to marinate properly.
5. Remove the salmon from the fridge and section the fish into 4 servings.
6. Use a large circle cookie cutter to lightly push the salmon into a thick patty using a spoon.
7. Remove the cookie cutter and garnish with a splash of olive oil and serve.

Baking Tips:

1. It is necessary to acquire fresh fish since this is a raw dish. If there is any skin on the salmon, it needs to be removed prior to cutting.

2. Take care when cutting the fish into cubes. If you cut them too small, the tartare will be mushy.

3. The marinating is not ultra-important to the dish, but it does help the ingredients to meld into each other properly.

KETO DESSERTS RECIPES

Chocó Chip Bars

Serves: 24

Preparation time: 10 minutes Cooking time: 35 minutes

Ingredients:

- 1 cup walnuts, chopped
- 1 ½ tsp baking powder
- 1 cup unsweetened chocolate chips
- 1 cup almond flour
- ¼ cup coconut flour
- 1 ½ tsp vanilla
- 5 eggs
- ½ cup butter
- 8 oz cream cheese
- 2 cups erythritol
- Pinch of salt

Directions:

1. 350 F/ 180 C should be the target when preheating oven.
2. Line cookie sheet with parchment paper and set aside.

3. Beat together butter, sweetener, vanilla, and cream cheese until smooth.

4. Add eggs and beat until well combined.

5. Add remaining ingredients and stir gently to combine.

6. The mixture should be transferred to the prepared cookie sheet and spread evenly.

7. Bake in preheated oven for 35 minutes.

8. Remove from oven and allow to cool completely.

9. Slice and serve.

Per Serving: Net Carbs: 2.6g; Calories: 207 Total Fat: 18.8 g; Saturated Fat: 8.5g

Protein: 5.5g; Carbs: 4.8g; Fiber: 2.2g; Sugar: 0.4g; Fat 83% / Protein 11% / Carbs 6%

CAKE

Expert: Crust-less Pumpkin Pie

Serves: 4

Preparation time: 10 minutes Cooking time: 30 minutes

Ingredients:

- 3 eggs
- 1/2 cup cream
- 1/2 cup unsweetened almond milk
- 1/2 cup pumpkin puree
- 1/2 tsp cinnamon
- 1 tsp vanilla
- 1/4 cup Swerve

Directions:

1. Preheat the oven to 350 F/ 180 C.
2. Spray a square baking dish with cooking spray and set aside.
3. In a large bowl, add all ingredients and whisk until smooth.
4. Pour pie mixture into the prepared dish and bake in preheated oven for 30 minutes.
5. Remove from oven and set aside to cool completely.
6. Place into the refrigerator for 1-2 hours.

7. Cut into the pieces and serve.

Per Serving: Net Carbs: 3.2g; Calories: 86; Total Fat: 5.5g; Saturated Fat: 2.1g

Protein: 4.9g; Carbs: 4.4g; Fiber: 1.2g; Sugar: 2g; Fat 60% / Protein 25% / Carbs 15%

CANDY: BEGINNER

Expert: Cheese Coconut Cookies

Serves: 15

Preparation time: 10 minutes Cooking time: 18 minutes

Ingredients:

- 1 egg
- 1/2 cup butter, softened
- 3 tbsp cream cheese, softened
- 1/2 cup coconut flour
- 1/2 tsp baking powder
- 1 tsp vanilla
- 1/2 cup erythritol
- Pinch of salt

Directions:

1. In a bowl, whisk together butter, erythritol, and cream cheese.
2. Add egg and vanilla and beat until smooth and creamy.
3. Add coconut flour, salt, and baking powder and beat until well combined.

4. Place mixture into the bowl and cover with parchment paper.

5. Place in refrigerator for 1 hour.

6. Preheat the oven to 350 F/ 180 C.

7. Spray a baking tray with cooking spray.

8. Remove cookie dough from refrigerator.

9. Make cookies from dough and place onto a baking tray.

10. Bake for 15-18 minutes or until lightly golden brown.

11. Remove from oven and set aside to cool completely.

12. Serve and enjoy.

Per Serving: Net Carbs: 0.3g; Calories: 68; Total Fat: 7.2g; Saturated Fat: 4.5g

Protein: 0.7g; Carbs: 0.5g; Fiber: 0.2g; Sugar: 0.1g; Fat 95% / Protein 4% / Carbs 1%

FROZEN DESSERT: BEGINNER

Expert: Classic Citrus Custard

Serves: 4

Preparation time: 10 minutes Cooking time: 10 minutes

Ingredients:

- 2 ½ cups heavy whipping cream
- ½ tsp orange extract
- 2 tbsp fresh lime juice
- ¼ cup fresh lemon juice
- ½ cup Swerve
- Pinch of salt

Directions:

1. Boil heavy whipping cream and sweetener in a saucepan for 5-6

minutes. Stir continuously.

2. Remove saucepan from heat and add orange extract, lime juice, lemon juice, and salt and mix well.

3. Pour custard mixture into ramekins.

4. Place ramekins in refrigerator for 6 hours.

5. Serve chilled and enjoy.

Per Serving: Net Carbs: 2.7g; Calories: 265; Total Fat: 27.9g; Saturated Fat: 17.4g

Protein: 1.7g; Carbs: 2.8g; Fiber: 0.1g; Sugar: 0.5g; Fat 94% / Protein 2% / Carbs 4%

Pumpkin Custard

Serves: 6

Preparation time: 10 minutes Cooking time: 40 minutes

Ingredients:

- 4 egg yolks
- ¾ cup coconut cream
- 1/8 tsp cloves
- 1/8 tsp ginger
- ½ tsp cinnamon
- 1 tsp liquid stevia
- 15 oz pumpkin puree

Directions:

1. Preheat the oven to 350 F/ 180 C.
2. In a large bowl, mix together pumpkin puree, cloves, ginger, cinnamon, and swerve.
3. Add egg yolks and beat until well combined.
4. Add coconut cream and stir well.
5. Pour mixture into the six ramekins.
6. Bake in preheated oven for 35-40 minutes.
7. Allow to cool completely then place in the refrigerator.
8. Serve chilled and enjoy.

Per Serving: Net Carbs: 5.2g; Calories: 130; Total Fat: 10.4g; Saturated Fat: 7.5g; Protein: 3.3g; Carbs: 8g; Fiber: 2.8g; Sugar: 3.4g; Fat 73% / Protein 11% / Carbs 16%

BREAKFAST RECIPES

Keto Avocado Pancakes

Preparation Time: 5 minutes Cooking Time: 10 minutes

Servings:4

Nutritional Values:

Fat: 16 g.

Protein: 7 g.

Carbs: 7 g.

Ingredients:

- 1 Large Avocado
- 2 Eggs
- ½ cup Milk
- ¼ cup Almond Flour
- ½ tsp Baking Powder
- 1 tbsp Erythritol

Directions:

1. Mix all ingredients in a blender.
2. Preheat a skillet and coat with non- stick spray.
3. Ladle in the batter and cook for 1-2 minutes per side.

LUNCH RECIPES

Flame broiled Portobello Mushrooms with Hummus and Feta Cheese

Complete: 20 min

Prep: 12 min

Cook: 8 min

Yield: 4 servings

Ingredients

- 4 huge portobello mushrooms
- Ocean salt, ideally dim ocean salt, and crisply ground dark pepper
- Olive Oil
- 1 (8-ounce) compartment hummus
- Feta cheddar
- 1 portion great dried up bread, cut into 4 areas

Bearings

1. Preheat the flame broil.
2. Fly out the come from the majority of your portobello mushrooms.
3. Season the two sides of mushrooms. Begin by showering olive oil (not all that much, only a slight sprinkle), some salt

99

and new dark pepper.

4. Cook mushrooms over a hot flame for around 4 minutes on each side.

5. In the meantime: Split the bits of bread, and haul out a portion of the delicate focus to make an opening for the mushroom burger. Spot the bread face down on the flame broil to toast.

6. Spot the mushroom burger in the bread, and top with a tablespoon of hummus and a lump of feta cheddar directly in the center and spread with a bit of bread.

SNACKS RECIPES

Garlic Breadsticks

Servings:8 breadsticks

Nutritional Values: Calories: 259.2, Total Fat: 24.7 g, Saturated Fat: 7.5 g, Carbs: 6.3 g, Sugars: 1.1 g, Protein: 7 g

Ingredients for the garlic butter:

- 1/4 cup Butter, softened
- 1 tsp Garlic Powder
- Ingredients:
- 2 cup Almond Flour
- 1/2 Tbsp Baking Powder
- 1 Tbsp Psyllium Husk Powder
- 1/4 tsp Salt
- 3 Tbsp Butter, melted
- 1 Egg
- 1/4 cup Boiling Water

Directions:

1. Preheat your oven to 400F / 200C.

2. Beat the garlic powder and butter and set aside to use it for brushing.

3. Combine the psyllium husk powder,

   baking powder, almond flour and salt. Add the butter along with the egg and mix until well combined.

4. Mix until dough forms using boiling water.

5. Divide into breadsticks.

6. Bake for 15 minutes. Brush the breadsticks with the garlic butter and bake for 5 more minutes.

7. Serve warm or allow to cool.

THE KETO LUNCH

Saturday: Lunch: Chicken Noodle-less Soup

All the comfort of a classic soup without the carbs. How comforting.

Variation tip: use the meat from a rotisserie chicken.

Prep Time: 10 minutes Cook Time: 20 minutes Serves 4

What's in it

- Butter (.25 cup)
- Celery (1 stalk)
- Mushrooms (3 ounces)
- Garlic, minced (1 clove)
- Dried minced onion (1 T)
- Dried parsley (1 t)
- Chicken stock (4 cups)
- Kosher salt (.5 t)
- Fresh ground pepper (.25 t)
- Carrot, chopped (1 qty)
- Chicken, cooked and diced (2.5 cups or 1.5 pounds of chicken breast)
- Cabbage, sliced (1 cups)

How it's made

Put large soup pot on medium heat and melt butter.

Slice the celery and mushrooms and add, along with dried onion to the pot.

Add parsley, broth, carrot, kosher salt and fresh pepper. Stir.

Simmer until veggies are tender.

Stir in cooked chicken and sliced cabbage. Simmer until cabbage is tender, about 8 to 12 minutes.

Net carbs: 4 grams Fat: 40 grams

Protein: 33 grams

Sugars: 1 gram

KETO AT DINNER

Saturday: Dinner:

"Breaded" Pork Chops

With crispy, keto friendly breading, this is sure to be a family favorite. Variation tip: if you can spare the calories, sprinkle with shredded Parmesan cheese.

Prep Time: 5 minutes Cook Time: 30 minutes

Serves 4

What's in it

- Boneless thin pork chops (4 qty)
- Psyllium husk powder (1 T)
- Kosher salt (.5 t)
- Paprika (.25 t)
- Garlic powder (.25 t)
- Onion powder (.25 t)
- Oregano (.25 t)

How it's made

1. Preheat oven to 350 degrees F.
2. Dry pork chops with a paper towel.
3. Combine the rest of the ingredients in a ziplock bag.

4. One at a time, seal the pork chops in the bag and shake to coat.

5. Put a wire rack on a baking sheet. Place pork chops on rack.

6. Bake in oven for approximately 30 minutes. The thermometer should read 145 degrees F.

7. Serve with vegetables or a green salad.

Net carbs: 0 grams

Fat: 9 grams

Protein: 28 grams

Sugars: 0 grams

Lightning Source UK Ltd.
Milton Keynes UK
UKHW012044170221
378908UK00003B/209